GREAT IS THY
Faithfulness

The Lord bless you + keep you,

Gillian

x

GREAT IS THY
Faithfulness

GILLIAN MOSS

authorHOUSE®

AuthorHouse™
1663 Liberty Drive
Bloomington, IN 47403
www.authorhouse.com
Phone: 1-800-839-8640

© 2013 by Gillian Moss. All rights reserved.

No part of this book may be reproduced, stored in a retrieval system, or transmitted by any means without the written permission of the author.

Published by AuthorHouse   04/15/2013

ISBN: 978-1-4817-8863-2 (sc)
ISBN: 978-1-4817-8864-9 (e)

Any people depicted in stock imagery provided by Thinkstock are models, and such images are being used for illustrative purposes only.
Certain stock imagery © Thinkstock.

This book is printed on acid-free paper.

Because of the dynamic nature of the Internet, any web addresses or links contained in this book may have changed since publication and may no longer be valid. The views expressed in this work are solely those of the author and do not necessarily reflect the views of the publisher, and the publisher hereby disclaims any responsibility for them.

Dedication

This book is dedicated to my friend Angie without whom this book may not have been written and I may not have discovered the goodness of God.

Chapter 1

Not just the first line of a well known hymn, but the truth of a loving, caring Father, wanting to be in every part of our lives.

Having passed my three score years and ten, I can look back over my life and see how He has been with me in so many ways and situations, both in good times and bad, and has truly proved to be faithful.

I would like to share some of these wonderful experiences with you. Sometimes I have been aware of His help or leading in very little ways that could so easily have been missed. Other times there have been quite amazing things happen where God was clearly speaking.

Our wonderful Heavenly Father still speaks to us ordinary mortals today as He did in days gone by, eg: dreams and sudden unexpected thoughts, (now where did that come from?), as well as by His Word, the Bible. He loves us all, unconditionally, whatever our skin colour or creed, or circumstances, abilities, (or lack of). After all, He created us in His own image, so the Bible tells us and, as with all else He created, He saw that it was good (see Genesis Iv31). He wants to be in a loving relationship with each and every one of us.

I was born on 30th November, 1939, which happened to be the day Russia declared war on Finland, so my mother told me. History was not my favourite subject at school, but that is one date that I will always remember.

We lived in a nice little house in the Pollards Hill area of Mitcham, in Surrey, now, I believe, classed as part of Greater London.

When I was about eighteen months old my father was called up to join the thousands of other young men who were sent to war to protect our country from invasion.

My mother and I moved to Tooting, in south west London, to live with her mother. Many children were evacuated to other parts of the U.K. and some were sent even farther afield to Canada and America. My mother chose to keep me with her as I was so young. We stayed in Tooting for the duration of the war.

Our home was damaged by bombs and we had to move. This happened on more than one occasion, and each time we had to find somewhere else to live, usually a flat or a couple of rooms, but once we managed to find a house I believe we lived in four or five different properties in less than five years. Praise God we were not killed, which was something of a miracle as friends and neighbours we knew well had lost their lives, or members of their families, and mother was often sad and tried to comfort them.

The worst time I remember was when I had woken up with bad earache and mother took me to see the doctor. He gave her some medicine for me and told her to take me home and put me to bed. According to my mother I was usually quite an obedient child, but this time I screamed and screamed and would not go upstairs. I remember it very clearly to this day. I just knew I shouldn't go upstairs and I was terrified. Minutes later a flying bomb fell nearby and the blast from the explosion took the whole of the top of our house, leaving just a pile of rubble in the back garden with my lovely dolls pram sitting on top looking a wreck. God was protecting us. There was thick brick dust everywhere and we had to cover our noses and mouths to be able to breathe. *I* was very upset about the loss of my doll's pram but mother promised to get me another one as soon as she could. I didn't realise it would be quite some time before that happened.

I started school at about the same time and I was very shy. If the siren sounded while I was at school, all the children were told to hide under their desks. Being so young we were not really frightened. Every day we had to line up with our teaspoons and the teacher would give each of us a spoonful of cod liver oil and malt. some of the children hated it but I loved it. We were also given a small bottle of milk each day. Each bottle held one third of a pint.

Everything was rationed during the war. I remember mother mixing the small amount of butter with lard to make it go further. Even sweets were rationed. I was given a Mars bar each week. This bar was cut into seven pieces, one piece for each day. It was a real treat.

Another time I remember an occurrence when the blast from another bomb blew the back door off its hinges and flung it across the kitchen, hitting my grandmother on the back of her head behind her ear. She had quite a deep cut and severe bleeding. Being a small child I was not really aware of the seriousness of what was happening and was completely fascinated by the downdraft of the blast coming from our coke range causing millions of sparks to fly across the room. I just sat there on my haunches pointing at the sparks crying ooh, ooh, ooh, as they flew past me.

Thankfully, neither mother or I were hurt. Just a few scratches only. Mother grabbed granny under one arm and me under the other and half dragged, half carried us out to the street. Our lovely President clock, which hung on the hall wall was down a hole where the front door mat should have been. It gave a mournful 'dong' as we stepped over it. Granny was taken to hospital to have stitches put in her head and be checked over but fortunately nothing else was wrong and she soon came back to us.

Every night, when mother put me to bed, (often in the Anderson shelter in the garden), we would pray and ask the Lord Jesus to take care of Daddy and bring him safely home again, when the war was over, which we also prayed would be soon.

It turned out that my father wasn't actually in the fighting for long as he, along with many other soldiers, was captured by the Japanese and was in various prison camps for the rest of the war. He was also made to labour on the Burma railway, nicknamed the 'Railway of Death', as so many soldiers died while working there.

He also spent a lot of time in another prison where some of the prisoners were treated very badly and tortured. Father said these were the ones who behaved badly towards the guards. Instead of causing trouble for himself he decided to make the best of it and keep out of trouble. Nobody likes war, and mostly the guards were reasonable. They too wanted it all to be over so they could go back to their own wives and families.

One of the guards saw my father looking at a photograph of my mother and me. He got out a photograph of his own wife and child and showed it to my father. Apparently the Japanese have a very high regard towards children. Over the time he was in that prison camp my father learnt quite a lot of Japanese.

When the war was finally over there was great excitement and celebration everywhere all over London and I expect all over the rest of the country as well. Bonfires were lit in the streets and everyone waved the Union Jack. There were street parties and such fun. Smiles and laughter on every face. Bread and jam and fish paste sandwiches. Jelly and blancmange. Jam tarts. What a feast! Today's children probably wouldn't think much of that, but when you hadn't had so much at one time for so long it was wonderful, especially considering what we had all been through.

Father did come home safely. Before the end of the war mother had said prayers with me every night and those prayers had been answered.

The day he came home I was the one to open the door to him. *I* was about six years old then. *I* recognised him straight away. He stood there in his uniform with his kitbag beside him. He looked like the photograph mother had kept beside my bed, only much thinner and a funny yellow colour. It had been four and a half years since I had seen him last, the day he went with all the other young men.

He came into the kitchen. Opened his kitbag and reached down inside to the very bottom. When he brought his hand out again, in it was a lovely big orange which he gave to me. He said he had picked it in Singapore before the journey home. It had been green then but was now a lovely ripe orange. I hadn't seen an orange for such a long time I couldn't remember ever having one before. How I enjoyed it. I gave some to Mum, Dad and Granny too.

As I have said, I was six years old when my father came home. Ten months later my mother gave birth to my baby sister. How delighted I was.

Chapter 2

All was well for a time. I adored my baby sister and enjoyed mothering her and playing with her. We were a happy little family.

Then things started to change, so slowly that I wasn't really aware of how it happened. Mother started working on Saturday mornings to bring in some extra income so that we could have a holiday and run a small car. We even had a refrigerator and a telephone, which not many people had then.

Little by little it started. Father played games with me while my sister was asleep. It wasn't until I was twelve years old and had sex education at school that I realised I was being abused, and had been since the age of eight! I now knew why I hadn't felt that what my father was doing to me was right, even though he kept reassuring me it was ok and was our special secret. I tried to make it all stop but then father was horrid to mother and threatened to harm her if I didn't comply, or told anyone about it. I became really scared after the day he banged mummy's head against the bathroom tiles one day after I had refused to allow him to touch me. Therefore things carried on as before and I became more and more miserable. Mum put my mood down to hormonal changes and I couldn't enlighten her.

I got to the point when I couldn't cope any longer. I was fifteen, almost sixteen, and I just had to tell someone, and make it all go away. I felt dirty and ashamed. I told a family friend who insisted we tell mother and promised that no harm would come to her.

To my humiliation and shame, and amazement, my mother's immediate reaction was to say 'it takes two'!! I felt bereft. The person I had been trying to protect for so many years just didn't understand or believe the degradation I had suffered, or the fear and stress.

I had started going to the local Baptist church with a friend. I went with a group from the church to hear Billy Graham, an evangelist from America, preach at Harringay Arena. There *I* heard the truth about the wonder of Jesus and how God had sent him into the world to save sinners and redeem them, forgive them and teach them how to live. I heard how He loved everybody and had given His life willingly so that we could have a relationship with our Heavenly Father. This is the kind of father I wanted. Billy Graham said how it was possible to become a child of God and have a new life.

All I had to do was give my life over to Him, seek His forgiveness and know that I would be loved and accepted and never be the same again. How I wanted that new life, so I rushed down to the front to give my sullied life to Jesus in exchange for a brand new one. Wonderful. I felt totally changed. The weight had been lifted from my shoulders. I knew without any doubt that what Billy Graham had said was completely true.

By this time my mother had made my father leave the family home and insisted that he see a psychiatrist. We moved from our lovely little house in Pollards Hill to a house in Streatham in south west London, only two miles away from my grandparents house in Tooting. Mother, quite understandably couldn't face the neighbours who would want to know why my father wasn't living with us anymore. He was away for two years and then mother allowed him to move back with us. He assured her he was completely cured and nothing like that would happen again. He didn't keep his word, but this time I decided to leave home myself so that mother wouldn't know and I would be free. I moved into a small bed-sit near where I worked and the lady was kind.

I had been very sad to leave my friends at church when we moved to Streatham. I was quite a shy person and I hadn't the courage to visit any of the local churches or make new friends. My sister was a very gregarious person who found it easy to make friends and also, as she was still at school, she was able to be with children of her own age.

Our house was very nice and mum soon made it into a real home. *I* had got a job and my sister was very happy at her new school. My job was with a handrail specialist firm. As I had learned typewriting and shorthand with a private tutor it seemed getting an office job was the best thing to do. Because of the predicament we were in back in Pollards Hill, I had had to leave school before taking my exams. I had always wanted to be a nurse but with no educational qualifications behind me it seemed out of the question now and mother had always wanted me to be a secretary, to follow in her footsteps.

I missed my church so much. I missed the preaching and the fellowship, and a sense of belonging. One night I was listening to my radio and somehow tuned in to Radio Luxembourg "Back to the Bible" at 10pm. How marvellous, now I could listen every night for my comfort and learning. How I enjoyed those messages.

One day my sister came home saying she had been to see the horses at the local riding school. We were both crazy about horses. *I* often went searching for more horse post cards to put on my bedroom wall. Not film stars or pop idols Strange child! I just had to go with my sister to visit these stables. I still had no real friends. The people at work were mostly a lot older than me. In fact I had been praying for a special friend with whom I could go to places instead of staying in all the time, as I was too shy to go anywhere alone. My sister and I went to the stables the next Saturday morning and there I met Diana who ran the stables. Diana turned out to be only one month older than me and we had such a lot in common We quickly became firm friends. It was as if we had known one another all our lives! The Lord had answered my prayers I was no longer alone, *I* had a friend. Praise Him. Over fifty years later we are still friends even though Diana now lives in Wales.

Chapter 3

I had wanted to be a nurse ever since I was three years old. I can remember my dear Great Grandmother, who I loved dearly, patiently allowing me to plaster her thick black stockings with Vaseline and bandage her up, time after time, and being given a nurses outfit for my sixth birthday.

Diana and I decided we would like to emigrate to New Zealand on the £10 assisted passage scheme. We went to New Zealand House in London to enquire how to go about it. We were told that I would be accepted but not Diana. Office workers were given passage but riding school mistresses were not needed in New Zealand. Our hopes were dashed and we left the building very downhearted.

A couple of days later I had a 'phone call from Diana asking me if I had ever considered becoming a nurse. What! Only all my life, but, being a stupidly timid creature, I wouldn't apply on my own and also not having any GCE's or RSA qualifications I didn't think I would be able to apply.

Diana's mother was a district nurse and she knew about applying. It turned out that a couple of fairly local hospitals would accept probationers if they passed an entrance exam in maths, english and I.Q.

We applied to both of the hospitals and fortunately we were both accepted at the same hospital. St. James Hospital, Balham. Sadly, St. James has been pulled down now and several blocks of flats put up in its place.

It was a great place to do our training and, despite the hard work, we thoroughly enjoyed ourselves. After three years training we both qualified as S.R.N's We could now go to New Zealand, or could we? Diana had been going out with a young man on a regular basis and instead of going to New Zealand she got married and moved to Cheam or Sutton, I can't quite remember which.

I stayed on at the hospital and I loved my work. I was very happy. God was always not far from my thoughts, and I would often pray silently for very sick patients, and even though I didn't go to church, I continued to listen to "Back to the Bible" whenever I could, and as my duties permitted, but not nearly as often *as I* had before.

Although I was relaxed and happy at work, I still found it difficult to mix with people in a social setting and usually refused invitations to parties etc. I have never felt very comfortable in that type of situation, even to this day, but one day I was coerced into attending a party in the doctor's home at the hospital. I didn't really want to go, but eventually agreed. I sat in a corner watching everyone else enjoying themselves. Occasionally getting up to take dirty dishes and glasses to the kitchen to wash up. I felt comfortable in the kitchen, but I couldn't stay there. I had to go back to join the others. How I wanted to disappear from that room and reappear in my own bedroom where I could be myself and relax.

I had noticed a rather quiet fellow sitting in another corner and looking just as uncomfortable as I felt. When I returned from the kitchen, he came over and said 'hello[1]. We got talking and found we had several things in common, like spending time in the countryside, animals, classical music and reading. We started going out together and eventually got engaged and then married.

Going back to our first meeting. Life can be very strange at times, can't it? It was a porter from the hospital who had encouraged me to go to the party in the first place. His name was John. Now would you believe it, another porter, whose name was also John, had encouraged Peter to go to the party! Peter's father was one of the doctors. I don't believe it was just coincidence that we met that way. I believe our lives are planned for us by our heavenly Father. We can choose to go our own way, but it is in our best interests to follow His leading.

Peter and I loved each other very much, but there was one important difference. He had been brought up in a home full of academics. He had been educated at public school, and both he and his two brothers were very intelligent. His father, as I have said already, was a hospital doctor. His mother was also very well educated. There was always wine by the case, and cider in the house, which was drunk every day. A lot of it!!

I was not used to this sort of life. My parents didn't drink, apart from a sherry at Christmas. They always bought a bottle to offer friends and neighbours who might call in. Peter was used to heavy drinking, and even after we were married he still drank heavily.

I soon realised that he had a problem, as after we moved to Brighton he would go to the local pub as soon as he got home from work, before having his dinner, and didn't return until closing time, having had far too many.

I felt that I should take some of the blame for his heavy drinking because, due to my childhood experiences, I was not the best wife in the world. Normal marital behaviour was very hard for me and even though I loved my husband very much I didn't want him to touch me. I clenched my fists, teeth and toes every time and just couldn't relax. It was very arduous for me and no pleasure for him. As I didn't seek help for my problem, indeed I didn't know if anyone could help me, I was trapped within myself. I dreaded that side of marriage and couldn't put my problem behind me.

We did manage to have two beautiful sons despite my reluctance, but our marriage was under a lot of strain. My husband was five years younger than me and I didn't realise that he had needs that *I* should fulfil. I had never discussed my hurt/problem from my childhood and I hadn't realised I might have been able to get help. Maybe it wasn't possible so much then. You never heard the word counselling.

Eventually my husband could cope no longer. He moved back to London to live with his mother. He came home occasionally but the gaps became longer and longer until he never returned. Every Friday evening I would sit at the window watching cars coming down the road, hoping that one of them would be Peter coming home. I often sat there watching and hoping until as late as 12 midnight or even 1 o'clock in the morning.

Chapter 4

Before Peter left me I had made friends with a young mother at my eldest sons pre-school nursery. She was a Christian and a very lovely person. She had three sons.

One day she asked me if I believed in God, to which I replied "Yes, no, I don't know". Although I had believed many years before, I had slowly let go of His hand, and had drifted away, without really being aware of it. I had let go of God, but He hadn't let go of me. Praise Him for His faithfulness when I certainly didn't deserve it. He had sent Angie into my life to bring me back into a relationship with Him again. Her question made me think, and after watching a film on television one evening a few days later, I realised that of course I believed in Him. Suddenly I wanted to get back to where I had been before and I started going to church again. Not a Baptist Church this time, but the nearest one to my home, which was the church Angie went to. It was an Evangelical Church of England. I wanted a relationship with the wonderful Jesus whom I had just been getting to know back in my teens. I was thirty-three.

Then began my exciting journey of learning more about Him and how I could get to know Him and trust Him with every part of my life. He loved me, Hallelujah!

When my husband had left me I not only felt worthless but also a complete failure to myself, to God and to my children. You know, God knows all about our lives and how they will turn out, what will happen to us and how we will react to such happenings. He knew my marriage was going to fail and He prepared me for that event by bringing Angie into my life as a way of reminding me He was still there and He hadn't forgotten me. *I* still praise Him for that. He knew how damaged I was and how to bring healing. Getting me into a loving fellowship of Christian women of my own age group and settling into a church where His Word was preached and taught really well, was the beginning of the healing process.

My friend had bought me a copy of The Living Bible and I devoured it. For a whole year I read and read and couldn't get enough of it. I joined the young wives group, where we met to study the Bible and pray together and enjoy one another's company.

I had noticed that they all seemed to have a special part of the Bible which meant a lot to them, a God given verse or verses. I wanted a special section for myself so I asked the Lord if He would please give me something, just for me, from His Word. I had the

Bible in front of me at the time and just sat quietly. Suddenly I wanted to read Psalm 34. I turned to it and read it. It was meant for me to keep as my own special piece of His Word. I was thrilled to bits and copied it out and stuck it on my kitchen wall where it stayed until it became faded and yellow.

My husband and I decided to try once more to save our marriage. A friend from church lent us his large campervan and we drove down to Devon for a few days, just the two of us. We left the children with my adopted sister.

Yes, we enjoyed our short break but it was clear that the intimate side of our marriage was not going to improve. Before we left Devon I went into St. Mary's church in Axminster and spent some time in prayer. I always like to put a donation in the box whenever I leave any church I go to away from home, but this time, when I opened my purse, there was only one 10p, two 2p's and the petrol money for the camper. I needed the 2p's for the telephone and *I* hadn't enough faith to put some of the petrol money in as the camper used a great deal of petrol as it was quite large and I didn't want to run the tank dry and cause damage to the engine. That only left the 10p! I talked to the Lord about it and apologised for my lack of faith in His provision if I put some of the petrol money in the box. I dropped the 10p in and left, feeling bad.

You know, we have such an amazing, loving and understanding God. Peter and I decided to stop and have our picnic lunch at Ford Abbey. After we had eaten we strolled through the wooded area, at the edge of which was some long grass. I kicked something which landed on the toe of my boot. What was it? you might ask. I could hardly believe my eyes, but there it was. A bright shiny, l0p piece! I felt truly humbled.

It was, to me, as if God was giving me back my l0p and saying to me, "There you are Gillian. You can keep your l0p, it's your heart that I want". Oh Lord, thank you for your patience with my lack of faith and know that you have my heart. I will always love You. Peter couldn't accept that it was anything to do with God. To him it was just coincidence, but I knew it was God.

I almost forgot to mention the amazing thing the Lord did for me without my even asking Him for help. Leastways, I cannot remember asking Him.

I had always had a phobia with regard to crane flies. I was absolutely terrified of them. Quite irrational, I know, but I just couldn't be anywhere near them. One camping holiday we used an old ex-army bell tent and one evening I saw several crane flies round the top of the pole inside the tent. I became paralysed with fear. I hid my face with my hands and begged Peter to get rid of them and take me straight back home. I was so frightened I can't even remember what happened next!

While in the campervan during that few days trying to save our marriage Peter said to me one evening, "Don't worry and sit quite still because there is a crane fly behind you on the window. I will get it out". I turned and looked, and sure enough there was a large crane fly just behind my head. I wasn't bothered at all and told Peter it was ok. He wouldn't believe I could just sit there so calmly with this large creature so close to me without making a big fuss as was usual. I believe that God had removed my fear out of compassion. I have never been afraid of them since. I can even catch them in my hands and take them outside if they come into the house.

Now, here is another time when I asked the Lord for help.

I didn't want a divorce. Being a Christian I didn't believe in divorce, but my husband was adamant that although he still loved me we had to go through with it. We couldn't go on as we were.

At my church there was a solicitor and I consulted him, and he agreed to take my case. Our divorce was so amicable that the solicitor agreed to work for both of us! I should think that would have been practically unheard of. After all we didn't hate one another, in fact we still loved one another, but just couldn't stay married.

I was still very unsure about going through with it, so one morning, before going to work as a district nurse, I sat with my Bible on my lap and told the Lord that unless He could show me in His Word that it was ok to allow the divorce to go through, I would do my very best to cancel the whole thing. I sat quietly for several minutes, then into my mind came 1 Corinthians chapter 7. I turned to it to find it was all about marriage and divorce. As no particular verse had come to mind I presumed I was meant to read the whole chapter, which I proceeded to do. When I got to verse fifteen, there was my answer. "But if the unbeliever departs, let him depart. A brother or a sister is not under bondage in such cases, for God has called us to peace". (KJV) My husband did not believe, and had no desire to do so, despite the fact that he had noticed the change in me since I had recommitted my life to the Lord, and liked the change. My faithful

Father had answered my prayer as I had requested and shown me, in His Word, that He allowed me to let my husband go.

Some time before my divorce I had been under a lot of pressure and was feeling very weary. My energy levels were at an all time low both physically and mentally. One particular day it all became too much and I cried to the Lord to refresh me and immediately the following words came into my mind and I quickly wrote them down:—

> Dearest Jesus, Prince of
> Peace, You never falter,
> never cease, to Guide
> me gently, day by day, As
> through life I wend my way.
>
> Though the path is often rough,
> Your light within me is enough,
> To let me know You go before,
> To smooth that path, my Precious Lord.
>
> I know I have my cross to bear,
> I also know that You are there,
> You lift its weight when oft I
> fall, And raise me up with
> gentle call.
>
> Beloved Comforter and Friend, I
> know You'll be there at the
> end. When life on earth has run
> its race, I long to see You,
> face to face.

I didn't work it out, it just flowed out and I quickly wrote it down. I immediately did feel refreshed and all weariness left me. I never needed to read those words again as they were permanently etched in my head and heart.

Chapter 5

My two sons and I moved to a smaller house. Peter had agreed to pay the mortgage if I could find the deposit. With this in mind *I* had worked for a nursing agency on my days off from district nursing. A friend looked after my children for a short while to help me. My elder son, Robin, went to a Christian school and was very happy there. My younger son, Adrian, was almost four years old the the school had agreed to take him as soon as he reached his fourth birthday. This they did.

After a while I had saved up enough money for the deposit on a house of our own. The house we had been living in belonged to my mother-in-law. It was lovely but very large and expensive to run, and needed a lot of work done, so mother-in-law had to sell it. With the deposit saved I looked around and soon found a suitable house for the boys and myself.

Peter stayed in London with his mother, which is where he had been living for the last couple of years. The new house had only a very small back garden, more like a yard really. This meant that I would no longer need my Flymo grass cutter as there wasn't any grass.

I knew I could move most of our belongings and small pieces of furniture to the new house myself as I had a small trailer, but I couldn't manage the freezer, or the piano, or the glass/china cabinet. I would need a removal van for those items. When coming to assess the cost of moving these items to the new address the charge was given as £17.50. As I didn't need the Flymo any more I decided to offer it to anyone in the church who might have use for it. Two friends came to collect it. They asked me how much I wanted for it but as I hadn't really thought about it I said whatever they wanted to give me. They offered me an envelope, in which they had put what the Lord had told them to give me. Imagine my surprise when I opened the envelope. Here, once again, my Lord was looking after me as, there in the envelope was £17.50, just what I needed to pay the removal men. Praise the Lord! I hadn't told anyone about needing a removal van, so there was no way my friends could have known how much I was going to have to pay them. Only God knew that. How marvellous He is. I really knew now how He cared about the little things in our lives, as well as the big things. Was He reminding me that although I had been rejected by my husband, He still loved me and wanted me to be assured of that? I believe so.

Not long after the boys and I moved to the new house following the divorce, I went through a very dry patch spiritually. I felt far from God, as if He had abandoned me. Of course I knew He hadn't, as His Word tells us He will never leave us or forsake us (Hebrews 13v5). I found it really hard to read my Bible or pray.

One evening, just after I had put Robin and Adrian to bed and was getting ready for bed myself, my telephone rang. It was a Christian friend of mine who was also a district nurse. She went to a different church from me as she lived in a totally different part of town. She had been having a prayer time and had felt a real burden and distinct nudge from the Holy Spirit to contact me. She said she had felt a heavy burden that had something to do with me. As she said these words I knew immediately what my problem was, and told her so. "I've got the flu" she told me, "so you may not want me to come round". "You come" I told her, "if God has told you I need help He's not going to let me catch the flu!"

Round she came and we sat in the living room while I told her how I was feeling. How *I* felt guilty about what had happened to me when I was a child, especially as my mother's first reaction was to say "it takes two". I felt that somehow it had all been my fault and I couldn't forgive myself, even though I knew that God had forgiven me all my sins once I had given my life to Jesus. My friend now realised why the Lord had sent her to me. She understood completely as she had had a similar experience herself.

I suddenly felt that I was being really arrogant. How dare I question the Lord's forgiveness; in doing so I was refusing His wonderful gift and putting myself higher that Him. How dare I question the Lord and Creator of the universe? With my friends encouragement I tried to pray. I said I was sorry but I needed confirmation from Him.

I went to bed feeling much more at peace and just left the problem with God. That night I had a dream that I was driving around in my Fiat 127, (which incidentally I had written off by falling asleep at the wheel while working both night and day to save enough money for the deposit on a house, and every other expense that comes with moving.)

In my dream I stopped outside a junk shop. A man with his leg in plaster was sitting in an armchair by the door. I walked past him and handed the lady, who was in the shop, a folded piece of paper. She unfolded it and read what was written. "This is of no relevance to me" she said as she handed it back to me. I then unfolded it myself and read the words Psalm 32, at which point I woke up. I knew exactly what the dream meant. The junk shop was my opinion of my life before I became a Christian. The people were my mother and father.

I quickly grabbed my Bible and opened it at Psalm 32 which begins "Blessed is the man whose transgressions are forgiven, whose sin is covered". It goes on to describe exactly how I was feeling. It then states He will guide me and watch over me. Praise You Lord. Thank You so much for answering my prayer so quickly and lifting the burden from my shoulders. Satan had been trying to convince me otherwise but God had not left me and He never would. It was 5.am and I was dancing around the bedroom praising the

Lord. I was back where *I* had been before, able to read the Word and pray, knowing that I belonged to God.

Life went on. I really enjoyed my job as a District Nurse. I loved the one to one care of my patients. I was reasonably happy, and not too lonely, as I still had my church and all my friends there.

Chapter 6

When I was a district nurse it was not easy for Robin and Adrian during the school holidays as I still had to work most of the time. My sister, who lived in Banbury then, used to have them for a week occasionally, which was nice for them and helpful for me.

Every so often we would all go to spend the weekend with her. The boys enjoyed seeing her two goats, which she kept at the local school, and also playing with her lovely Welsh collie called Tessa.

We went to see her one weekend when Tessa was due to have her pups. Linda's house was full of people that weekend. Altogether there were fourteen of us all anxious to see the new arrivals, if they came on time, as anticipated. Tessa duly went into labour and most of the adults and children kept out of the room while Tessa was giving birth. I stayed with Linda in case Tessa needed help. It was her first litter so we gently encouraged her and rubbed her back and talked soothingly to her. Eventually the puppies arrived. Five of them in fairly quick succession. All had been spoken for but my boys begged me to let them have one. I didn't want the responsibility of a young pup. It was hard enough having two boys to worry about in working hours. As it appeared there were no more puppies to come I said to the boys that if Tessa produced another one we would have it, not expecting there to be another one. However, about one and a half hours later Tessa's head shot up and there was a surprised look on her face. She turned to look at her rear end and, well I never, there was pup number six. A perfect looking collie with beautiful markings, including a big white ruff. I wished I could have eaten my words. Here was the promised pup. Oh dear! One of Linda's friends who was going to have one of the puppies immediately asked if she could have that one as she had always wanted a perfectly marked collie. I felt I couldn't refuse as we weren't going to have one originally. I chose another one instead.

Back home in Brighton the boys looked forward excitedly to the day we could collect our puppy. Six weeks later I received a letter from my sister saying that the pup we had chosen had developed brown markings as well as the black and white ones. She was a tricolour. Linda's other friend had asked for a tricolour, should there be one in the litter. The other pups were three dogs, all spoken for, and the remaining bitch, the runt of the litter. My sister had named her Little Nell.

By this time I had rather gone off the idea of having a pup anyway but when I spoke to the boys they were really upset. They couldn't understand why we couldn't have the puppy we had chosen and begged me to insist on keeping the tricolour. Now, the particular friend of my sister who wanted the tricolour was not a well person. She was really nice, but was living on borrowed time. She had several serious things wrong with her including a chest problem/ a heart problem and a blood problem, and her spine was badly curved. I couldn't refuse to let her have something she really wanted could I? I did my best to explain to the boys. I told them that I believed that if we did the right thing and gave the puppy we wanted to her, and we had the puppy that no-one wanted, then God would bless us and our puppy would turn out to be the best one after all.

I'm glad to be able to say the Lord did bless us. Little Nell, or Jess, as we renamed her, turned out to be *a* really lovely dog and we had her for seventeen and a half years. Unfortunately, the perfectly marked pup, called Sharna, had to be put down as she became completely neurotic and unable to be trained. She spent all day chasing shadows and imaginary things and couldn't be left alone.

The tri-colour, Gwen, got run over by a train when she was about eighteen months old. So sad, and so devastating for their owners. I had watched them grow up and they were both lovely dogs. I found it hard to believe they had both gone.

Jess was a joy. She loved coming to work with me, guarding the car if necessary, when I was with a patient. If I had a few minutes to spare I would take her to the nearest park and play ball. She loved chasing the ball.

When David and I got married, he not only had to accept my son, but my dog and cat as well. He already had a cat, but there was no problem. They all got on well. Jess loved being taken to the local woods, as most dogs do, and early morning was the best time. While she ran about enjoying herself with the various smells, I spent time with the Lord. We all missed her very much when we had to let her go. I vowed never to have another dog as I didn't want to go through such a painful time again. Losing our cats was bad enough, but losing Jess was indescribable. I have had many cats, rabbits, and other small furry animals, and the passing of each one is painful but the loss of Jess was just too much. I couldn't go through that again.

Chapter 7

At the beginning of August 1978, I took the boys and my adopted sister Mary to our first ever Bible Week, at Harrogate, in Yorkshire. It was amazing. Several thousand people from home and abroad gathered together in tents and caravans, meeting together every day in seminars or the main meeting area for preaching and teaching. The children had their own meetings. We all had an amazing time despite the terrible weather that year. Thunderstorms and torrential rain all week, which most people were not prepared for, but we all made the best of it. Many of us improvised with black bin bags for raincoats having cut holes for head and arms. We stayed fairly dry. When the ground became too muddy some of us resorted to bare feet at times.

One night the wind was so bad that some of the tents were blown away, and some caravan awnings were ripped off, never to be seen again, but very few people went home. Those who were still secure made room for those in need and the camaraderie was everywhere, which bound us all closer together. That was the year that angels were seen in one of the main meetings. Unfortunately I had missed that particular meeting for some reason, so had not seen them myself, but many had and couldn't stop talking about it. That was the same day that Robin had given his heart to the Lord. He was almost nine years old. Adrian had given his heart to the Lord several months earlier just after his sixth birthday.

On the evening of the 'offering' I felt the Holy Spirit prompting me to give £25. I didn't like that idea as I knew that when we got back home the gas, electricity and telephone bills were all due. Back in 1978 £25 was quite a lot of money, considerably more than it is today. "Have I not promised to supply all your need?", "Yes Lord. Lord I will do as You ask and I trust You with the bills." The day following our return home, my parents came to visit. This was an unusual occurrence. They still lived in Streatham and were very busy with the Sequence Dance club they ran. I handed my father a cup of tea and at the same time he handed me a folded piece of paper. It was a cheque for £1,000. God keeps His promises. The bills duly arrived and I had more than enough to pay them. Hallelujah!

Towards the end of the Bible Week, some people were being baptised in a tank of water. Somehow I hadn't heard about it so I missed the opportunity. I really wanted to get baptised so much and was upset I had missed it.

When back in Brighton I learned that people were going to be baptised in a local church. Not our church as it was Church of England and didn't have a baptistry. I very nearly missed the chance again. I had to wait for a friend to come and stay with my children and as she was late I had to run all the way to the church. Thankfully it was downhill all the way. *I* got there in time and was duly baptised and prayed for. I came up out of the water crying with joy that I had made it.

I remember the Pastor saying that the Lord would do exceedingly, abundantly, more than I could ask or imagine in my life. How true that prophecy was. God has blessed me far more than I deserve or could ever have imagined, but He has also taught me a great deal through hardship and heartache. 2 Corinthians 4vl7-18 says, "For our light affliction and momentary troubles are achieving for us an eternal glory that far outweighs them all. So we fix our eyes not on what is seen, but on what is unseen. For what is seen is temporary, but what is not seen is eternal". God keeps His promises.

Chapter 8

The last week in August that same year, we were supposed to be going on holiday with a friend of mine and her two boys. We had a small campervan and a tent, and we were going to stay on a dairy farm in Devon where we had been several times before. Just a few days before we were due to go my friend telephoned to say her car had broken down and she couldn't afford to have it repaired and also to go away with us. She was sorry, but she would have to cancel.

I didn't fancy taking my children on my own so I told them we wouldn't be going after all. They had been looking forward to it so much. They loved camping on the farm. After much pleading on their part, and feelings of guilt on mine, *I* finally gave in and said we would go after all. I decided I had better get used to the idea of being on my own without a husband. After my divorce I had said to the Lord that I was not going to get married again unless He wanted me to. If He did want me to then He would have to bring the man direct to my door and make it very clear to me. Little did I know He would do just that a few months later.

For some time there had been a verse in the Bible, in Luke, that really bothered me. It was Luke 14v26 where Jesus says in the King James version, "If anyone comes to me and does not hate his father and mother, his wife and children, his brothers and sisters—yes, even his own life he cannot be my disciple". How I struggled with that verse. I wanted to obey Jesus but this verse appeared to be asking too much. I kept praying about this verse. How could I hate my own family, my beloved children?

One day I read the same verse in the Living New Testament. "Anyone who wants to be my follower must love me far more that he does his own father, mother, wife, children, brothers, sisters—yes, more than his own life—otherwise he cannot be my disciple". In a nutshell, put Jesus first before everybody and everything else. This I would endeavour to do even though it would be difficult, but much easier than being told to hate everyone dear to me. I just hoped He wouldn't put me to the test. He did.

The boys and I set off for Devon very early on the Saturday morning. I'm the sort of person who likes to get to my destination in time for breakfast so as not to miss any precious time of our holiday.

We arrived at about 8.30am at Lyme Regis in Dorset, which was not far from the part of Devon we were heading for. There was a store there which sold all sorts of things so we went in and had a look around. Among other things *I* bought a small dinghy

GREAT IS THY Faithfulness

for the boys. While we were in the store my Robin asked me three very significant questions, which, at the time I didn't think too much about as, if you are a parent, you know that children often ask unusual questions right out of the blue.

The first question was, "Mummy, does God tell you when you are going to die?" I was a district nurse at the time and, on more than one occasion, a patient had said to me, "Sister, I won't be here when you come back on Monday Sure enough they had passed away during my weekend off. My answer to Robin was, "I believe so Robin". A few minutes went by, then he asked, "Mummy, when I die will Jesus come and take me up to heaven?". I considered this for a moment then said, "All over the world people are dying at the same time, and although we know Jesus is everywhere by His Spirit, He can't be everywhere in person, so I would imagine He will send an angel for you and will be waiting in heaven to meet you". This seemed to satisfy him then, after several more minutes had passed he said, "Mummy what's it like to die?". That was a much more difficult question to answer, but I did my best by replying, "I don't know Robin, I've never died but it's going to be ok as the scriptures say He will be with you in the valley of the shadow of death, and in heaven there is no crying, or pain, or suffering of any kind, so we know everything will be fine. There's nothing to worry about". He pondered this and seemed satisfied as there were no further questions.

Three days later we decided to take a picnic and go to Charmouth beach as it was such a lovely day, warm and sunny. Robin was really happy that day, and he went skipping along ahead of Adrian and me, singing a little song he had learned at the Bible Week. The words were:—

> Something good is going to happen
> today, happen today, happen today,
> Something good is going to happen
> today, Jesus of Nazareth is coming my
> way.

Little did I know that would be the last time I would hear him sing.

We arrived at our chosen spot on the beach and spread out the blanket. Our collie dog, Jess, was just as excited as the children. The boys could hardly wait to get into the water so I quickly put the swim—safe on Adrian. This was the first time he had been allowed in the water due to having grommets in both ears. He hadn't been able to learn to swim yet because of this. Robin, on the other hand, was an excellent swimmer. He had private lessons and his coach had said, only the week before, what fantastic stamina he had for a nine year old. Robin was not going to wear a swim—safe, so I didn't press him. After all, they were only going to be at the waters edge.

They were both sensible boys, so I shortened the painter enough so that Robin could pull Adrian along in the shallow water. They were both so excited and happy as they ran down the beach, dragging the dinghy behind them.

GREAT IS THY faithfulness

Adrian climbed in and Robin started to pull him along just a little way from the shore.

I was keeping an eye on them in between writing post cards and throwing pebbles for Jess to catch. For a time all was well. They were having a wonderful time. On such a lovely day the beach was crowded with people and the sea was full of swimmers, dinghies, lilos, rubber tyres, etc. Everyone was having a marvellous time. *I* wrote another postcard and this time, when I looked up, the boys were a little further out. I jumped to my feet and called to them to come back. Many boats and people were much further out than they were but I didn't want them going any deeper.

Sitting next to me were another couple. The man asked me if there was something wrong to which I replied "Yes, my children, they're going too far out". "Don't worry" he said, "I'll get them for you". He had only gone a short distance when he turned and came back. "I'm sorry", he said "I can't" Then he told me about the shelf. When the tide is in you can't see the shelf caused by the tide pushing the sand and shingle up the beach into a ridge. The water suddenly becomes deep. The boys must have discovered they were in deeper water, but Robin, being a good swimmer, was not afraid and he just held on to the side of the dinghy and pushed Adrian along by kicking his legs, just as I had done with both of them round Lyme Regis harbour only three days before. I was not able to swim myself, but I knew I was quite safe as long as I held on to the dinghy. Robin was just copying me.

There was an off shore breeze that day. An oh so gentle breeze, you hardly noticed it. My dinghy, with my two sons, was being slowly taken out to sea. The wife of the man who had tried to get the boys for me told me to stay and watch them while she ran down the beach to where a fishing boat was about to launch, just beyond where the river Char entered the sea in a trickling stream. She asked them to help and I saw her point to where my children were.

As the boat left the shore, my Robin let go of the dinghy and started to swim for shore. I still had no fear as I knew what a good little swimmer he was. He had only gone a few strokes when I saw him founder and disappear from view. The current was too strong for him.

Everything he had asked me three days before, and the little song he had sung that morning, came rushing back into my mind. Oh no! "Father, save him", I prayed, "But if it is not your will to save him, then give me the grace to bear it". I stood on that beach unable to do anything to help my child, but trust in God, who never makes mistakes. His ways are not our ways, and He knows the reasons He allows seemingly bad things to happen to us. I then had the most amazing experience, which I find impossible to describe properly. It was wonderful. It was as if the Lord Himself had come down and wrapped His arms around me.

I felt comfort and at peace, and totally wrapped in love.

I watched the little fishing boat reach Adrian and pluck him out of the water. It circled round a few times but couldn't find Robin. As they were heading back to shore I ran along the beach to where they were coming in. I have very sensitive feet and find it very hard to walk on pebbles, let alone run, and Charmouth is a mixture of sand and pebbles. I ran and didn't feel a thing. It was as if my feet didn't touch the ground.

When I arrived at where the fishing boat was I discovered someone had sent for the coastguard. He asked if someone was in trouble in the sea, to which I replied, "Yes, my son has just drowned out there"[1] pointing to where it had happened. At that moment I was completely calm. The chap from the fishing boat handed me a very white faced Adrian.

In minutes the Lyme Regis life boat was scrambled and even a helicopter with three frogmen began searching too. The frogmen jumped out of the helicopter and began diving and searching for three hours. Police were walking up and down the beach with loud hailers calling out Robin's name, and I remember thinking, Why are they doing that, I told them I had seen him drown.

There was a free-lance photographer who asked me if he could take our photographs and I refused. A policeman put Adrian and me in the ambulance for privacy, but it was too late, the photographer had already taken the pictures before asking permission and they, with an account of the tragedy, appeared in all the local and national press the very next day.

While Adrian and I were waiting in the ambulance, the doctor from the lifeboat came to see me. He was very kind, and upset that their efforts had been fruitless. They had been unable to find Robin. I looked at him quite calmly and said "You were not meant to find him". The poor man must have thought

I had flipped, but I knew that my precious Robin's life on earth was finished. The Bible tells us that there is an appointed time to be born, and also an appointed time to die. Our lives are in God's hands, and it is entirely up to Him how long each one of us is given on earth. One day we will know perhaps, but it is not up to us to question.

Chapter 9

Early in my married life I had lost two babies. One by miscarriage at three months following an ovarian cystectomy. The doctor thought the baby was ectopic, but it was perfectly fine. He took the cyst out but unfortunately, because of the surgical interference and the strong painkilling drugs I had been given, the baby couldn't cope and it died.

I then had Robin, but I very nearly lost him too. I kept bleeding and had to stay on bed rest for several weeks. I did manage to keep him, thankfully, and he was born on 12th August 1969. After Robin I lost another baby. This one died inside me at twenty weeks. At that time it was thought too dangerous to remove the dead foetus and you were just left to abort naturally, which I did at 27weeks. As you can imagine, it was not very comfortable emotionally having to carry your dead baby inside you for several weeks.

The nurses did not sympathise with me on the loss of my baby, only the fact that if I had managed to hold on to it for one more week I would have been eligible for the maternity allowance! That was the last thing on my mind. I just wanted to get back home to my Robin.

These days, in that situation, the doctors take you into hospital and remove the dead child. I had my Adrian a couple of years later in 1972. I should have had four sons, but here I was with only one. Thank God I still have him.

Going back to the day I lost Robin, the police kindly took Adrian in a police car to give him something else to think about, and another policeman drove my campervan for me as I was now feeling very shaky and nauseated, and I didn't think I could drive.

They took us back to the farm and told our friends what had happened. Our friends had a visitor and I felt very uncomfortable and awkward sitting in their kitchen. I'm sure it wasn't easy for them either. I knew I had to try and keep myself in check for Adrian's sake, but all I wanted to do was let the pain out. The pain of losing my precious firstborn son. To lose a child must be the worst possible pain in the world. Your heart literally does ache, and no amount of painkillers will take that pain away.

Eventually I could stand it no longer. I went to the outside toilet and hit the wall, and cried and cried. I was not angry with God, that came later and is a normal part of the grieving process. Thankfully it didn't last long, but I just had to let all the anguish out. Adrian was just very pale and quiet. I don't think I did a very good job of comforting him.

We slept in the farmhouse that night and although I wanted to stay in Devon, hoping Robin's body would be found, a 'phone call from the police in Streatham, from my parents house, encouraged me to go home to be with them. I didn't want to go, but what else could I do? I couldn't stay at the farm, and our holiday was well and truly over. As well as me losing a son and Adrian losing his brother, my parents had lost a grandson.

Could anything get worse, or add to our suffering? Well it would appear so. As I was driving back to Streatham, my campervan oil light came on. Into the first garage I came to, I went, and topped up the oil. Off we went again, only for the same thing to happen a few miles further on. This pattern was to repeat itself throughout the journey, several times. When we reached Balham, which was a couple of miles from my parents house, *I* pulled in for the last time, and promptly burst into tears. I had come to the end of myself. I was tired and distressed, and felt I couldn't go on any longer. The mechanic wanted to know why I was in such a state. When I poured out the whole story to him, he was very kind. He made me a cup of coffee and filled up the oil reservoir with used oil so *I* could get to my parents house. He told me the cause of the trouble was the timing chain had gone which caused the oil to leak out.

Adrian and I stayed at my parents house for a few days. My father arranged for my car to be repaired. My ex-husband came and we wept together and I felt so sad for him because he hadn't the wonderful knowledge that I had. I shared with him exactly what had happened, but he did not want to believe. To him,

Jesus was just a good man who had lived a couple of thousand years ago, not the son of the Most High, creator of the universe.

Five days later, my Robin's body was washed up on the same beach at Charmouth. A mother who had been pulling her son, who had learning difficulties, along in a little dinghy near the edge of the water, stopped short when her son cried out "Mummy, look" and there was Robin floating face down only a few yards away. A man who was walking his dog came over and pulled Robin from the sea and up onto the beach, then covered him with the dinghy and called the police. I sometimes think how distressing it must have been for them, and I thank God they were there at just the right time, on that very section of the beach. You know, as the Bible says, God's timing is always perfect.

At the inquest I met all the people who had been involved in the tragedy. The couple who had been sitting beside me on the beach. The couple from the fishing boat, and the lady whose son saw Robin's body in the water. They were all there and we hugged one another and I was able to thank them for their part in it all.

Writing this, all the memories come flooding back and the tears fall. Anyone who has lost a child will know the pain never goes away completely, you just learn to live with it. It gives you understanding when you hear of people going through a similar trial and you can get alongside them and offer comfort as you really do know what they are going through. If not able to do so in person, any form of communication is a help.

I know my beloved Robin is happy where he is, and to me, it is as if he had just moved to another country, far away. Somewhere I couldn't afford to go and visit him, but I knew he was alive and well. He has just changed his address, and one day, when my time comes, I will see him again. Oh, what joy that will bring.

When Adrian and I got back to Brighton, (Hove actually) we carried on the same routine as we had done when Robin was with us. Every night, at bedtime, I would read Bible stories to Adrian and we would sing children's choruses. Then we would pray together. The only difference being I would keep Adrian up for an hour longer, and go to bed myself an hour earlier. That way I didn't sit and brood by myself.

Chapter 10

One of the names of Jesus is Healer. At one time, when he was only a baby, my son Adrian had suffered with deafness due to glue ear, and he had two sets of grommets inserted at different times, without any real improvement. His hearing was well below normal.

I arrived home from work one evening to find a flyer on the mat saying there was going to be a healing service at the local Pentecostal church that very evening. I decided to go and take Adrian along. I had been to the family planning clinic that morning to have an intrauterine device removed from my womb as I no longer needed it. When the doctor took it out she told me to go and see my GP as soon as possible as there were lumps and bumps in my uterus which shouldn't be there. Before making an appointment I decided to go to the healing service myself. Adrian and *I* duly went that evening.

When we arrived at the church we were given cards on which to write our problems, and hand them to the gentleman who was the channel of healing power so that he could lay hands on us and pray for us. Neither Adrian or myself were aware of anything happening, but when I went to see my GP the next day he told me there was nothing wrong with my uterus. It was perfectly normal. Praise the Lord, He had healed me.

The following week Adrian had an appointment at the throat and ear hospital for a hearing check up. The result showed that, for the first time in his life, his hearing was within normal limits. "Hallelujah". Neither of us had any further problems. This was in 1978, not long after the Lord took Robin.

One night, after saying prayers with Adrian I was kneeling beside my bed and saying my own prayers. Suddenly I was aware of a little figure kneeling beside me. When I had finished praying I turned to Adrian and asked him what he wanted. "Mummy", he said, "Can we pray to Jesus and ask Him for a new Daddy, and some brothers and sisters 'cos I'm so lonely?". "Ok son" I replied, and then "Lord Jesus, you've heard Adrian's request, so if it is your will, please could you send a man into my life who would be a good father to Adrian, and be my spiritual head. Please could he also have some children".

A few weeks later I thought it might have been prudent to be a bit more specific about the number of children!!

I thought no more about that prayer, and life carried on as before. Then one day a friend came round and brought me a copy of the Argus, our local newspaper, so that I could look through the used car section. My old campervan was spending more time in the garage for repair than I liked, and I had to keep borrowing a council vehicle for my work as a district nurse. I really needed a more reliable vehicle.

I didn't get the chance to look for a car that evening as we were talking and having a meal together, but after she had gone I picked up the paper, which my friend had left on the floor open at the used car section and folded in half. Now, I am left handed. Had I been right handed I would have picked the paper up with the used car section facing me, but, being left handed, as I picked the paper up from the floor the page opposite the used car section was the first thing I saw.

There, in the middle of the page, in bold black type, was an advertisement. I couldn't miss it. It read:—Lonely widower, young family, seeks Christian woman for friendship". My heart went out to this man who had lost his wife and had been left to bring up his children alone. Before I realised what I was doing I grabbed a pen and paper and wrote "Dear friend in Jesus"

I told him what had happened to me and how I understood something of what he was going through. Round to the Post box I went and dropped the letter in. My goodness, what was I doing? I never even glance at the personal column in the paper, let alone answer an advertisement, and here I was, having done that very thing. Too late. I couldn't retrieve the letter. What was I going to do? Oh well, just forget about it, I told myself, nothing will come of it, so there is no need to worry, and back home I went.

This was about the end of October 1978. What an eventful year it had proved to be, and it wasn't over yet! My divorce finalised in the February, Robin becoming a Christian at the beginning of August at the Bible week and then going to be with the Lord at the end of August. Then answering the advertisement in the paper, which I wouldn't normally do. What was going to happen next, I wondered.

A week or so later I had my answer. I received a letter, written in a very nice hand, from a man called David. It was in reply to my letter to the post box in the local paper. It was a very nice letter in which David explained his circumstances and how he came to be in them. Apparently his first wife had left him and gone off with someone else, leaving him with four children. After trying to get her back, to no avail, he devoted himself to looking after the children. Four years later he had met and married a lovely lady called Barbara, whom he adored, as did the children, especially as they had been without a mother for so long. Shortly after their marriage Barbara found that she was pregnant and both of them were absolutely delighted. She so wanted a baby of her own. For a short while everything was wonderful, especially as it turned out she was expecting twins.

It was then discovered that Barbara had breast cancer. The family's world tumbled about them. The whole family was knocked sideways. This couldn't be happening, especially as they had been so happy. David clung to his faith and immersed himself in the scriptures. The whole family prayed for Barbara's healing. As she had so desperately wanted children of her own she refused treatment, hoping that once the children were born she could then commence treatment and get well.

By the time the twins, two lovely boys, were born, Barbara's condition was beyond any chance of remission, and she went to be with the Lord when they were four months old. David and Barbara's marriage had lasted just thirteen months. David was on his own again. This time with six children, two of them just four months old. His other children's faith took a hard knock. They had fully believed that Barbara would recover, but God had taken her. Why?

God, who sees the end from the beginning, and who never makes mistakes, has His own reasons for allowing us to go through difficult times. He allows us to go through difficult ordeals. Times of tribulation and trial while we are on planet Earth, because He sees the bigger picture. How can those who have never suffered or lost in other ways identify with others who are going through similar ordeals. How can those who have had a comparatively easy life, with no hard difficulties, troubles or pain understand those who do.

Trials and tribulations are a part of life and help to strengthen us, so hang in there if you are going through such times at the moment. Things will get better in time. Praise God, not only for the good things that happen, but also for the bad. Remember Romans 8v28, "and we know that in all things God works for the good of those who love Him, who have been called according to His purpose" (NIV). That means <u>ALL THINGS.</u> Just trust Him with whatever happens in your life. He will not fail you. Even if you have to wait, what would seem a very long time. God's timing *is* always perfect, and He is a loving Father. His timing is different from the way we think of time. Sometimes He doesn't answer in the way we want Him to. If that is the case, He has something better for us. We just have to trust and wait.

Chapter 11

I finally agreed to meet David after speaking to him on the telephone. I had given him my number when I replied to his letter. He had a really nice voice and I enjoyed talking to him.

We decided to meet at my house where we could chat over a cup of coffee. I felt more comfortable in my own surroundings. Of course he had to bring the twins with him. They were four years old at the time.

When I opened my front door and saw these two little boys with scarves wrapped around their faces, and woolly pom-pom hats pulled down to cover their foreheads, all I could see were two pairs of big brown bewildered looking eyes staring up at me. I was lost. I bent down and gathered them into my arms. It was November, and very cold. We went indoors and there began our friendship which soon blossomed into love.

I started popping round to see David and the twins some afternoons, when *I* had an hour or two to spare. We often went to the park and the boys played on the swings and slide while David and I talked. Once a week David would get the older children to look after the twins while he cycled over to my house and had a meal with me. We would spend the evening together. We felt very comfortable in each others company.

There was a young man at my church who was recovering from a nervous breakdown and I was helping him by going to clean his flat for him once a week, doing his laundry, and baking him the odd pie. In return he would often take me out to lunch, and once a week he would take me Scottish country dancing, which I really enjoyed.

I took this fellow with me one Christmas to stay with my sister, who had moved to mid-Wales. While we were there I had a lovely letter from David, telling me what fun they had been having in the park, with all the snow, and how much he missed me.

It was a very cold winter, both in England and Wales that year. In Wales the snow was so deep you could hardly see where the gates to the fields were as you literally stepped over them.

On return to Sussex I called round to see David and the twins. I hadn't met any of the older children yet as they were either at school or at work. We were both so pleased to see one another. The following day David telephoned me in the evening and asked me to marry him. I said yes immediately and knew it was the correct answer because a warm feeling went right through me from the top of my head to my toes. Again I said yes. David could hardly believe it and wanted to come round straight away.

What I am going to tell you now, I know you will have difficulty believing, because even though it actually happened to me, I have difficulty believing it myself.

Not long after I had accepted David's proposal my telephone rang again. This time it was my ex-husband. I told him my news and he was not happy. He said I hadn't asked his permission, and if I was going to marry anyone I should get re-married to him. I told him I believed what I was doing was the right thing. I believed it was what God wanted me to do.

The very next morning early, at about 5.am, just as I was leaving for work, the telephone rang again. It was the fellow I had taken to Wales with me and had been friends with for several months. He was ringing to ask me to marry him. In fact his words were, 'would I consider becoming his wife'! What was going on?!! Now come on, I was no beauty, just a very ordinary person. No-one gets three proposals in less than twenty-four hours. I decided that I had very definitely made the right decision in saying yes to David (after all God had brought him directly to my door as I had asked in my prayer several months before), and that Satan was trying to throw a spanner in the works and confuse me. He is a deceiver ever and delights in trying to mess up our lives. He hates it when people try to follow the Lord's leading.

Having made my decision I must admit I was a bit scared I had explained to David that I had a problem and came with unwanted excess baggage, but he said that was ok and we could work it out. Another reason I was scared was the children. *I* was fine with the twins, they were so young and had never known their own mother and I was very happy to fulfil that position. But what about the other children? Their ages were 13, 15, 17, and 22. I had never been allowed to be a normal teenager myself. I never went out with friends, except to go to the home of one particular friend where we sat like a couple of old ladies doing knitting or sewing. Can you imagine the teenage girls of today doing that?!

On just one occasion we went to the pictures together to see Doris Day in Dance Around the Daffodils. The film didn't finish until 10pm and I was supposed to be home by 9.30pm. I got a dreadful telling off for being late. I was fifteen at the time.

I didn't know how to cope with teenagers. What was *I* going to do? Again God was one jump ahead of me. He had it all worked out, so what was I worrying about. I called to see David one day, and one of the children had a bad cold and was home from school that day. Another time the teachers had an inset day so another child was home, so I had now met two teenagers. They weren't so scary after all. The seventeen year old I didn't meet until Boxing Day. It was a brief meeting as he went straight up to his room and put his music on, LOUD. How I met the eldest daughter I cannot recall, and neither can anyone else. I do remember that she did all the catering for our wedding, and she must have worked very hard. Anyway, I gradually met them all and we got on fine. What a relief.

We had a small wedding at the Baptist church where David was a member. I would have liked to get married at my own church, but as it was Church of

England it was not possible as I had been divorced. I didn't feel it was right for us to worship at different churches, so I left my church and joined David. I did miss my own church and hardly saw any of my friends any more as my life was now so very different. I had nine of us to look after, plus my own dog and cat and David's cat.

I stopped working as a district nurse, which I really found hard, but my new family needed me and there was no time for outside work or interests now. I would be telling lies if I said life was wonderful from the beginning. It was extremely hard. Suddenly becoming a stepmother to so many children was no easy task, especially as they still remembered Barbara, and had put her on a pedestal. I'm sure she was a really lovely person and I realised she was a hard act to follow. I tried to do the best I could. I didn't want to take her place in the children's hearts, I just wanted to earn my own small place.

I didn't want to be thought of as the wicked step mother, so any changes I wanted to make had to be made very gradually and carefully. Have you ever tried to get your own children to keep their rooms tidy? Put their dirty washing in the bin, or help with the washing up? Believe me, it is far harder when you have arrived on the scene with mid-teenagers.

The first two years of our marriage were really hard for me, and many a time I felt like picking up my son, my dog and my cat, getting in my campervan (I never did get rid of it), and going—heaven knows where! BUT I did know I was where the Lord wanted me to be, and I clung to Him for strength and grace, and stayed put. Thank God I did, because everything eventually fell into place, and now I couldn't be happier.

Immediately after our wedding David was able to go back to work with Seeboard, where he had been before the loss of Barbara. That was a minor miracle in itself. He applied for his old job as a meter reader, and a vacancy had just come up, so they took him back straight away. Wonderful! At least one of us was working now.

Chapter 12

We rented the house we lived in and the rent was very low, but the house itself left much to be desired. It was very tatty indeed, and I must admit I found it quite depressing and did what I could to improve things.

I had only been married to David for a few months when I developed depression. I think so much had happened to me in such a short time that something had to give. My life had changed so much and although I believed I was where God wanted me to be, I still found it very hard.

I felt a bit like Cinderella. There was just so much to do, and I wasn't able to see my friends. I missed my Robin very much indeed, as did Adrian. He got on really well with the twins, which was a good thing, but I had to take him away from his school where Robin had been because the twins went to a school just ten minutes walk away and it wasn't possible to take the children to two different schools.

I forced myself to get the children to school every morning and then returned home to sit and stare into space for hours. My adopted sister, Mary, came round every day to help me. I didn't tell David how I was feeling because I didn't want him to worry, but one day he was working locally and popped home for lunch. He saw me sitting at the table just staring into space, and Mary with me. When she told him I had been like that for several weeks he went straight round to the doctor's surgery and made an appointment for me to be seen.

I duly went for the appointment and saw a very nice lady doctor. I promptly burst into tears and poured out everything that had happened to me over the past year or so. She wasn't a bit surprised that *I* was depressed and gave me some medication which she thought would help me. She also made a follow up appointment. Gradually I returned to my former self and was fine for a couple of months, then it all came back again. Back on the medication I went and again soon recovered, only for the same thing to happen again after a short period of time. This was not good.

I remembered I had read several books by Merlin Caruthers about praise, and how praising God changes things, so I decided I would follow his leading and start praising God. In his books he had said that even if we don't feel like praising, we have free will and we can choose to praise. I certainly didn't feel like praising but, if it might help me, with my will I was going to. Firstly, I told God I didn't feel like praising but with my will I was going to try, so would He please forgive my lack of depth of feeling. Normally *I* loved praising the Lord, and I didn't like the way I was now.

Every morning I spent time reading the Praise psalms aloud so that I was hearing as well as seeing the words. I then praised Him for everything I could think of. A roof over my head, water on tap, a comfortable bed, enough food, clothing, my dear husband, my children, my pets, birds, trees, flowers, but most of all the fact that Jesus died for me and forgave all my sins and loved me. I went on and on, not forgetting my dear Mary who came every day to support me.

After about two weeks I realised I wasn't feeling so bad. I kept praising and soon felt completely well again. I still had the odd bout of depression but each time I praised the Lord until they were gone. Eventually I had no more depression at all. I'm so glad I took Merlin's advice.

Chapter 13

My sister Linda had lived in Banbury, Oxfordshire, for a couple of years. Her husband Alan was a postman. Together they decided to move to Wales if Alan could get a transfer. It was not long before the transfer came through, and off they went.

Not long after they moved to Wales my parents also moved there. My sister wanted us to move there as well, but it was not to be. At that time David and I didn't want to take the children from their school as exams were looming, and the older ones had a year or two before finishing senior school. We decided to wait until they had left school, and the younger ones would be in junior school.

Instead, we bought a static caravan on a site very close to my parents bungalow to enable us to visit them during the school holidays. This worked very well, and the children loved visiting Wales.

We had been married about three years when we had a telephone call from my parents telling us my sister had been killed in a road traffic accident. She had been on her way to feed her animals. She had two goats, a few sheep, and some ducks and hens, which she kept in a field she rented from a local farmer. She had always wanted her own smallholding. To get to her field she had to ride her moped down a very narrow, winding lane, which had high hedges on either side as most Welsh lanes do. This particular morning she was a few minutes earlier than her usual time.

As she approached a sharp bend, a car coming in the opposite direction knocked her off her moped and smashed her right leg. The young man driving was used to passing her in the lane, but not so far down it as she was that morning. It must have been a terrible shock to both of them.

My sister had four children, the youngest being only two years old. The others were in their teens. Another family tragedy. I went down to Wales to be with them all until after the funeral. I went on my own as David couldn't leave the children.

Even in this circumstance God was helping me. I wanted so much to be able to do something to help my sister, but what could I do? I asked the Lord, and once again He heard and answered me. My sister's husband asked if I and my sister's friend Maxine would like to go with him to feed the animals. Of course we both said we would.

When we got there, one of the goats was very restless. She was pregnant and I thought she might be ready to give birth, but Alan said she wasn't due for another ten days. He said we should go back and have our breakfast, but Maxine and I decided to stay with the goat, just in case we were right. It was a good thing we did because a short while later it was very obvious that she was in labour and the kid was going to be born. We watched and waited. Then suddenly one hoof appeared. I knew it should have been two hooves and a nose, something wasn't right. Nothing happened for several minutes, then the nose presented, but still only one hoof. I sent Maxine to get the farmer and meanwhile I washed my hands and arms to see if I could help. In between contractions I got hold of the goats tail with one hand and gently pushed the nose and hoof back into the birth canal. I located the other hoof and eased it round into the correct position beside the first one. Fortunately I have very small hands so it was easy to do. I then eased both hooves and nose as the goat pushed and the little kid slid out into my arms. I cried with joy. Had I not been there that goat could have been in serious trouble and torn herself badly. God had answered my prayer. I had been able to do something for my sister after all. Hallelujah! Shortly after that the goat produced a second kid all by herself. She had had twins.

Chapter 14

We had only been married a few months and had just returned from a lovely holiday camping on the Isle of Wight, when I was woken up, in the early hours of the morning, by stertorous breathing coming from the bedroom where the younger children slept. I went in to discover one of the twins was very unwell. Richard had a high temperature and was very swollen. He needed a doctor urgently. While David telephoned the G.P, I proceeded to sponge him down, and gave him a drink of water and a paracetamol tablet to try to bring his temperature down.

When the doctor arrived she wasn't quite sure what was wrong so she went to the surgery to check in her medical books. Her initial diagnosis of Nephritis was correct. Richard had a severe infection of the kidneys.

As we had a car, she suggested we take him to the children's hospital ourselves as it would be quicker than sending for an ambulance. The children's hospital was only five minutes away, and in the middle of the night there wouldn't be much traffic.

He was a very sick little boy and it was touch and go for several days. How I prayed. I couldn't believe God was going to take another child from me. He wouldn't do that, would He? It was August. The same month that Robin had been taken the previous year. I stayed with Richard as much as I could, only leaving him to dash home to cook an evening meal for the rest of the family. Back to the hospital to spend the night on a camp bed beside Richard, then back home again in the morning just long enough to get the other children off to school. Mercifully, Richard eventually began to recover. What a relief that was. He was soon back to his normal self and playing with his brothers again.

As Richard grew he remained well, apart from falling off the top bunk bed and breaking his collar bone one time, but he never looked really well. His skin was a different colour from his twin brother. Whereas Robert always looked pink and healthy, Richard looked sallow and everyone in the family thought he looked ill. He assured us he felt absolutely fine.

He left home when a young adult in his twenties and lived in a flat with one of his elder brothers. He had gone through a broken engagement and was feeling very depressed and lost. One night he came to our house after we had gone to bed and, not wanting to wake us, he had slept in our porch. It was an open porch and it was winter and very cold and snowy.

My next door neighbour telephoned us at six-thirty in the morning to say there had been a young man sleeping in our porch all night. She thought it was one of the homeless people who come to our church every Monday evening to get *a* hot meal and clothes. She hadn't recognised Richard as it was very dark and he had a hat and scarf on, which hid most of his face.

Straightaway I rushed downstairs to the front door and invited the young man in out of the cold. As he slowly got to his feet and removed the scarf, I realised it was our Richard! David came downstairs and I managed to get a cup of tea into Richard, who was very cold and in a dazed state, but I had to feed him with it as he couldn't hold the cup. We took him upstairs and put him in our bed having removed his very cold trousers and wrapped him in a blanket. Our bed was still warm.

We telephoned for an ambulance as we thought Richard must be suffering from hypothermia. I had found an open notebook in the top of his rucksack, which he had left open with the notebook on top. He had obviously wanted us to read it. He had written how he was feeling—several pages, and it was a cry for help.

When the ambulance arrived we gave them the notebook. They checked for hypothermia, which was confirmed, and rushed us all to the hospital.

Richard was checked over thoroughly and one of the blood results showed a very low platelet count.

The doctors were more concerned with his mental state so didn't follow that up. It was a couple of weeks later, when Richard was recovering and staying with us, that one of the psychiatric nurses asked me if *I* was worried about anything. I was very worried about his low platelet count and told her so. She arranged for his G.P. to visit the next day. The G.P. took more blood samples.

Following these tests and scans, it was discovered that Richard had Cirrhosis of the liver and also lots of small blood clots in the veins between his liver and spleen. This was a shock to all of us as Richard had never been a heavy drinker and you usually associate Cirrhosis with drink.

He went back to his flat and a few months later he rang us late one evening about 10pm to say he was feeling nauseated and had just coughed up some blood. He was going to take himself to A&E. David told me to stay in bed as I had been up since 3.30 that morning, and he would meet Richard at the hospital, which he did.

A short while later he telephoned me to tell me to get to the hospital as quickly as I could as Richard had had a massive haemorrhage, and the doctors were literally fighting to save his life. Oh, help Lord!!

As David had taken the car I had to take a taxi. On arriving at the hospital David and I were put in a side room to await events. We put everything in God's hands, and waited. After, what seemed like an eternity, one of the doctors came and told us they had managed to stop the bleeding, but at this stage they didn't know what the outcome would be. They had had to give him eleven pints of blood, and put him in an induced coma and on life support. He was kept under very heavy sedation for three days. Further blood tests showed his vital organs were all working ok, which was a great relief to both of us, and also to the doctors.

On the third day, in the afternoon, we were visiting him in intensive care when the doctors decided to slowly wake him up. It was a tense few minutes as no-one knew if he had suffered any brain damage, or if he would be ok. Thank God, he opened his eyes and recognised us. We were sent out of the room while he was disconnected from the life support machine.

When we were called back into the room it was wonderful to hear him speak, albeit rather croakily. The haemorrhage had been due to ruptured oesophageal varices. For a long time Richard had to make regular visits to the hospital for the varices to be banded to prevent them from rupturing.

Richard was referred to King's College Hospital, in London, for further investigations. As he has a very low platelet count it doesn't make sense that he had blood clots. The doctors have done many investigations to try to get to the root of the trouble but, no matter how many tests they do it seems they are rather baffled. All they can do is treat the symptoms. Richard has bouts of severe pain which the doctors treat with morphia. Even though he is on warfarin he is still developing clots. We are very proud of him as he never makes a fuss and just gets on with life. He has a very supportive girl friend as well as his family behind him.

Chapter 15

Adrian found it very hard to cope with the loss of his elder brother and blamed himself. He felt he should have saved him, but he was only six years old at the time, and unable to swim. I tried to reassure him but he couldn't accept it. He kept saying there was a rope in the boat which he should have thrown to Robin. What he called a rope was just a thin nylon cord which he wouldn't have been able to throw at all, it was too light.

One Sunday morning, in church, a man got up and said he had a word for someone. The picture he described was exactly as Adrian was feeling, so he knew it was meant for him. He was in his late teens then. He went and talked to the chap after the service and subsequently had counselling for about six months. Counselling did help a bit but the pain didn't go completely and I know it never will. He has learnt to live with it as I have. *I* pray for him regularly.

Going back to our house. After we had been married two or three years and our rented house had been sold over our heads three times in two years, we decided to try and buy the house ourselves. Having a succession of new landlords just wasn't very reassuring, and they never wanted to spend money on the property. We had rain coming through the roof in three places, in three different rooms. It wasn't until rain came through the light fitting in our bedroom ceiling, and trickled onto our bed so that David had to go up into the loft at 3am to tack a piece of plastic to the beams to catch the water, that we were given a new roof. Because of the neglect the house had to be rewired as well.

When we told the agent we would like to buy the house ourselves he came round to inspect it. His opinion was that the only people this house was of any value to was ourselves He agreed to talk to the new owners. They agreed to sell to us, but at a figure two thousand pounds more than they had paid for it only two months before, quite a profit for them.

Back then house prices were not nearly as expensive as they are today, and as we were sitting tenants we got a really good deal.

I was sure we could manage to pay for it if David would let me go back to work. The children were all either at school all day, or at work, so I felt I could manage if *I* did night duty which paid more. I would be there when the children came home from school and David would be there at night. I went to work for four nights a week, which meant we were able to afford a mortgage.

It was so good not having to show prospective buyers over the house any more and having to answer their questions which were only asked to find out how much rent they could obtain from us. What is more, we could now do some improvements, and the first thing we did was to get an extension on the mortgage to put in a new kitchen. At last, a decent kitchen to work in. What a pleasure that was.

Little by little we re-decorated the house inside and out. We had double glazed windows put in the front as the old sash windows rattled so badly when it was windy and we had to stuff newspaper down the sides. When it was very windy the bedroom door would slam and then join in the rattling.

In the winter ice would form on the inside of the windows and the whole house was very cold. We would go up to the local woods and collect fallen branches for the fire. Once the house was ours and I was working, we had a gas fire installed in the sitting room which was wonderful. No more tramping up to the woods. We then added electric storage heaters, one at a time. How lovely it was to have a warm home at last.

Chapter 16

A few years later my father became very ill with emphysema. He had been in and out of hospital several times and had to have oxygen and a nebuliser at home every day, to help him breathe.

Our telephone rang about one o'clock in the morning in the dead of winter. It was the hospital saying that my father was really poorly and we should go to be with my mother. Things were not too desperate, but it was a long way to go, and they knew we wanted to be there should the worst happen.

We left straight away and arrived at mother's bungalow around breakfast time. The weather was very bad. We had to drive through a blizzard to get to Wales, and could hardly see the road. It was a bit scary, but we got there safely.

The journey to the hospital was nineteen miles over a narrow mountain road with a sheer drop on one side and steep mountain on the other. When we arrived we were surprised to see father sitting up in bed drinking a cup of tea. He recognised us all but was talking about seeing spiders, and it wasn't a real hospital but a film set. He was hallucinating due to the lack of oxygen to the brain.

We stayed at the hospital for several hours but mother was getting quite distressed so David took her home. I stayed with father. He kept trying to get out of bed and it was all I could do to stop him. He was in a side ward so he wasn't disturbing other patients. Eventually a couple of male nurses came and settled him down again, but not for long. He was soon up again, trying to get out of bed, and getting very distressed, which was upsetting for me. The nurses sent for the doctor who explained to me that there wasn't anything they could do for him except give him a mild sedative, which would help to calm him down, which I knew already. The sedative might make it more difficult for him to breathe. I said I realised that, but as they couldn't make him better, I would like them to at least make him more comfortable. I think the doctor gave him a valium tablet. After a while he was sleeping peacefully and breathing regularly with no difficulty.

One of the nurses had seen me reading my Bible and asked me if I would like a minister of religion to come. I asked if he could get in touch with the vicar from the local church, whom I knew well, and ask him to come. About three quarters of an hour later, Trevor arrived. *I* was so glad to see him.

We went into another room and the nurse brought us both a cup of coffee. I shared with Trevor all that had happened when I was a child. I had forgiven my father but I didn't want him to die without God's forgiveness. This worried me a great deal. We prayed together and then went back to my father, who was sleeping peacefully. You would not have known there was anything wrong with him, there was no difficulty breathing at all and his skin was normal looking, not pale. Trevor gave him the last rites and as he said lay not their sins to their charge, my father suddenly took a deep breath, let it out slowly, and was gone! Hallelujah! Trevor and I grinned at one another and thanked God. Father had been forgiven, of that there was no doubt.

Unbeknown to us, one of the nurses had been watching from the doorway. He came into the room and said "I hope you don't mind my being here, but I have just witnessed a miracle. Your father was nowhere near the point of death. Your prayers have been answered". God is good. He knew how much I wanted my father to be forgiven, so He showed me he had. Praise the Lord, yet again.

Trevor then drove me back to my mother's over that dangerous mountain road. It was very treacherous, so icy and foggy, but we were not afraid.

Not wanting to wake my mother, I went round to the back of the bungalow and tapped on the window of the room where David was sleeping. *I* was still so excited over what had happened, and was just bursting to tell him.

Chapter 17

One Sunday morning I woke with a very painful back. I had suffered with back ache on and off for some time but this particular morning it was more painful than usual.

It happened at the time when the Holy Spirit was being very active in our church. Several people had been healed of different problems or just blessed with the Spirit's touch. During the service I asked Jesus if he would please heal my back. I didn't want to be falling down when He touched me. I asked Him to please do something different this time if He was going to touch me. Our Lord had a good sense of humour. A call was given for people with back problems to go to the front to be prayed for. Several of us made our way forward and were prayed for in turn.

When it was my turn, I was determined I wasn't going down, but God had other ideas. As I was prayed for it was as if I had been punched in the stomach. All the air whooshed out of me and I found myself sitting on the floor! I could sense the Lord laughing at me, as if to say, 'who's in charge here, you or me?' Needless to say my back pain disappeared and for some time I was fine.

After several months my back started to trouble me again. This time much worse than before, so I went to see my G.P. who sent me to the hospital to see a specialist. X-rays were taken and when I went for the result I was told I had osteoporosis. There were two collapsed vertebrae in my spine. I was in most pain at night and I couldn't sleep without strong painkillers. It was hard to turn over and I certainly couldn't have a lie-in as it was so uncomfortable. David had to push me out of bed in the mornings because it hurt too much to get up without help. During the service on Sunday mornings I couldn't stand for longer than about ten minutes or so before I had to sit down. It didn't feel right sitting down but I wasn't able to participate as I had done before.

A gentleman called Ram Babu came to our church from India. He was a man much used by God both in winning people for Christ and also for healing. The first year he came I went forward but I wasn't healed.

The second year he came there were quite a few people with back problems, about twenty in all. We went to the front to be prayed for, but this time Ram Babu just held out his hands over us and prayed a blanket prayer. Initially I was a bit disappointed that he hadn't laid hands on us individually as he had before, then I realised that my back wasn't hurting, and when he asked us to do something we hadn't been able to do before, I found I was able to bend every which way and there was no pain or stiffness at all. Wonderful, I had been healed. Thank You Lord yet again, You are so good. I went to bed that night without pain and slept really well, without painkillers, for the first time in six years. The next morning I didn't need help getting out of bed. Oh, hallelujah! I really don't deserve such goodness to me. I am so glad You are in my life. Please continue to work in my life, by the power of your Holy Spirit, and make me more like You.

Everything was absolutely fine for three days, and then the pain came back badly. How could this be? God had healed me. There should be no pain. I decided I wasn't going to accept this, as I believed it was Satan trying to convince me I hadn't been healed. Well, I knew Satan was a liar and a deceiver and I felt the only way to send him packing would be to quote the truth of scripture at him, which I did. Every morning and evening for about two weeks I reminded him that he had no dominion over me. I am a child of the King. When Jesus died on that cross, He not only took my sins but also my diseases, and the word says that by His stripes I am healed. Then one day I realised that the pain had gone, this time for good. Satan cannot stand under God's Word.

Chapter 18

Another time, I remember, when scripture came to my aid was when my mother had been behaving rather strangely toward me. I was feeling rather upset and confused and rejected. It had been several months since my father had died. Her short term memory was getting bad. It had been getting worse so I made a point of writing to her every week and telephoning her every week-end. I also drove down to see her every six weeks and stayed for a long week-end, making sure she had plenty of food in the freezer etc. Gradually she became more and more cool towards me until one time, when I went to see her, I noticed all the photographs she had of me had disappeared from their usual places and were not to be seen anywhere. Gone from the top of the piano, gone from the sideboard where they had been for years and years. When I questioned her about it all my mother would say was 'don't you know?' I had no idea why. I had always done all I could do to help her. What more could I have done?.

Driving back to Brighton one very stormy day after one of these weekends and feeling very dejected, I pulled into a lay-by and had a good cry. Then I remembered Psalm 27 verse 10. "Though my father and mother forsake me the Lord will take me up"(KJV). Immediately I felt better, and drove on.

No wonder we are told in the Bible to 'let the Word of God dwell in you richly' (Col 3vl6) It is such a blessing to us. We certainly can find help in time of need, as the Holy Spirit brings verses to our remembrance.

I am very glad to be able to say that that difficult time eventually passed. I had brought Mum home with me to have a little holiday, which she really enjoyed. She stayed a fortnight and then decided to go back home to Wales as 'she didn't want to impose'.

We had just reached the outskirts of Wales when she suddenly decided she had made a mistake and wanted to come back with me to Brighton and live with us permanently. I was really pleased about this change of heart because it meant no more worries for me, being so far away from her. We had our back room downstairs redecorated and made into a nice bed-sitting room for her. There was even room for her beloved piano, which she loved to play every day. She was a very good pianist. She left the London College of Music with honours. She was able to play right up to a few weeks before she died.

We managed to get a second-hand stair lift put in for her. This enabled her to go up to the bathroom. As she had very severe osteoarthritis she was not able to manage stairs, and walked slowly with a Zimmer frame.

After Mum had been with us a couple of months or so, she decided to sell her little bungalow in Wales as she wouldn't be going back there. She very kindly offered to pay off the remainder of our mortgage, which was a real blessing as, unbeknown to us, David was going to be made redundant the following year. The redundancy payment would not be enough to pay the mortgage. Without Mum's help we would have been in a bit of a predicament. How very grateful we were to her.

Mum lived with us for six years in which time she accepted Jesus as her Lord and Saviour. She went to be with Him and the age of ninety-one.

Chapter 19

David and I have always loved camping and we had some lovely times. When the children were young we had a seven berth tent to accommodate us all and spent one marvellous three weeks on the Isle of Wight where it didn't rain once. We were there for Cowes week regatta and the firework display at the end of the week were absolutely breathtaking. All the children were open mouthed in wonder at the size and magnificence of them all. A real treat to see.

Once all the children had flown the nest, apart from one of the twins, (our Robert has learning difficulties,)

we bought a two berth folding caravan and have had some lovely holidays with it. So much easier to erect than the seven berth tent, which, of course we didn't need any more. Robert often comes with us and he has his own pop-up tent. What a marvellous invention, it virtually erects itself!

We had a lovely holiday one year. We did a two thousand mile trip up the east coast of England, staying a couple of nights in the Lake District, followed by a tour of Scotland camping at some great places. I really love the mountains, waterfalls and trees, and superb views. Scotland is really beautiful. In fact, in my opinion, there is no more beautiful country in the world than Great Britain.

One summer we were camping on a farm in Suffolk. It was a lovely warm summers day, Midsummer's day in fact, and we were just sitting and enjoying the peace and natural countryside sounds. I suddenly found myself inspired to write what I saw and heard. The owners of the camp site liked the poem so much they still have it on the wall in the communal area of the facilities block several years later! Perhaps you would like to read it:-

MIDSUMMERS DAY AT LONELY FARM

> The bees collecting nectar from the clover. The rabbits playing over near the hedge. The birds that sing and sing 'til day is over, And Moorhens feed beside the water's edge. The butterflies that dip, and dart, and hover. The pheasant's plumage, and it's barking cry. The golden sun that warms the earth, and ever white fluffy clouds play chase across the sky.

> With these delightful things dear Lord, You bless us,
> And we are ever grateful for Your care.
> Help us to always give, as You have blessed us,
> For You have given all your gifts to share.
> On such a day as this, in these surroundings,
> All worries flee, and peace doth fill my soul.
> For troubles, though they come, are only passing.
> You give us strength to overcome them all.

Some years ago David and I were taking a few days holiday in our little folding caravan. We weren't able to go for long holidays any more as we only had our pensions which were enough pay for everyday things but there wasn't much left for anything else. If anything went wrong with the car we would be in trouble and might have to get rid of it. We needed it to pull the caravan. As my son, Adrian, lived in North Yorkshire with his wife and two little boys we needed it to go and visit them at least twice a year. As they lived in a lovely village it would be difficult to go out together as six of us wouldn't fit in their car, seven of us when Robert came as well.

it was difficult for them to visit us as the boys were very young and it was too long a journey, plus the fact that we didn't have accommodation for them all. The house which once had practically burst at the seams with nine of us, (ten of us for a while as a friend of one of our sons had been thrown out by his parents and had moved in with us for twenty-two months), had had some alterations to the place. We had knocked the downstairs rooms into a through lounge, and one of the bedrooms had become our 'Den[1], containing my sewing machine, our computer and David's model railway, among other things.

On travelling back to Brighton after one of these visits I decided to try and get a little job so that we could have a little spare cash. As I was six and a half years younger than David, it seemed only right that I should be the one to work.

I didn't mind what kind of work. I just wanted to work for a few hours a week. I asked the Lord if He would kindly provide some sort of work for me.

When we went to church the very next day I could hardly believe it when I saw a flyer in the news sheet saying a part-time cleaner was required for the Clarendon Centre, which was where our church gathered. I quickly applied for the job and, although our congregation was very large, around 8-900 people, no-one else applied. The job was mine, Hallelujah! Thank You Lord. Once again He had answered my prayer. The Bible does say that He knows what we need before we ask Him (Matt, 6v8).

I did the job for seven years, which was the amount of time I had decided I wanted to work for. I would be seventy-one then. I felt seven was a good biblical number. I really enjoyed doing it although the last two years I found it quite hard due to my physical condition. I had had atrial fibrillation since I was fifty-eight years old and at first it didn't bother me very much, but as the years passed it became a nuisance, and other problems compounded the trouble. I made many visits to A&E. I had several things done to me over the years including being shocked back into rhythm, and something called ablation, where a nerve in the heart is burnt, to hopefully stop the fibrillation which was happening very frequently and lasting for nearly twenty-four hours at a time. Nothing worked. Eventually there were longer and longer gaps every few minutes when my heart stopped beating, and I had to lie down quickly before I fell down!

I went to A&E again one Wednesday, but by the time I was seen, everything had calmed down, and I was back to normal. The doctor did lots of tests but couldn't find anything wrong with me and had to send me home. He said to me that although he couldn't find any problem, if I still felt unwell, I was to go back. I was fine the next day, no problems at all. The day after I just had a few attacks so let it pass. On the Saturday I was ok again but on the Sunday morning I was feeling horrible. Fibrillating badly then feeling really dizzy and having to put my head down quickly. This was happening just the same as the previous Wednesday when I had gone to A&E. I knew I wouldn't be able to go to church, I just wanted to go back to bed, but thankfully David insisted I go back to the hospital as the doctor had told me to. To my surprise the same doctor was there. Over all the years I had been visiting A&E I had never seen the same doctor twice!

Would you believe it, by the time the doctor came to see me everything had calmed down again. What would he say? Bless him, he decided I should be kept in overnight and arranged for the cardiac team to keep an eye on me. This was in spite of the fact he couldn't find anything wrong with me again. He said that despite things seeming to be ok he chose to believe the patient.

A doctor from the cardiac department came and sat beside me and said *I* would be sent home in the morning because I wasn't ill enough to be kept in hospital. Ok, whatever you say. I dozed off only to wake at 2.30am with four people round my bed. The portable defibrillator and oxygen cylinder on the bed and I was being moved! I was told I was being taken to the Cardiac Unit. That's odd, I thought. Bit of a waste of a bed, I'm being sent home in the morning!

Once on the ward things really began to hot up. I kept waking up violently shaking and unable to speak. This happened several times and the next thing I knew I was being rushed to cardiac theatres to have an emergency pacemaker fitted. I was told by one of the nurses later that my heart had kept stopping for eight seconds at a time which caused me to fit due to lack of oxygen to the brain. How I thanked God for that wonderful doctor in A&E. If it wasn't for him I would have been sent home and it could have been quite a different story. I probably wouldn't be writing about it!

Chapter 20

When my two sons were small I had made friends with a girl a few years younger than myself. She loved my boys, and they loved her. After we had been friends for awhile it became obvious that she had very little self confidence and found it very difficult to interact with more than one person at a time. She would also take offence very easily so you had to be careful what you said to her. She also appeared to have a learning disability.

As she had no family of her own, having lost her parents, I decided to adopt her as my sister. Not legally you understand, but I gave her a piece of paper on which I had written that I had adopted her, and whatever life threw at us I would always be there for her. My mother adopted her also. That was over forty years ago.

Since that time she has been a great blessing to me in many ways.

When David and I first got married and had very little money and a large family, she would often come round to visit us and she never came empty handed. Sometimes she would bring meat of some sort, or fruit, or vegetables. She even went to the sales and bought tee-shirts or trousers or some other item of clothing for the three younger children.

It was only because of her generosity that I was able to keep the camper. It was she who taxed it and insured it to keep it on the road. She also often paid to put petrol in the tank as well. Without the camper we wouldn't have been able to on our camping holidays. Of course we often took her with us.

In 2008 she suffered a severe stroke and lost all feeling down the right hand side of her body, from the top of her head right down to her toes. Although she hadn't lost movement. She can walk a little with my help and the aid of a stick, but very slowly. She has some speech loss as well, initially it was quite bad but now she is able to converse somewhat. It is very frustrating for her when the wrong words come out and she can't say what she means. Her short term memory is not very good now. She has very little control over her right arm as muscles in her back go into spasm causing the arm to thrash around and twist her body to the right. These spasms are quite painful at times and are more pronounced if she is worried about anything.

Following the stroke she was in hospital for over three months altogether. Soon after being transferred to another hospital for rehabilitation she developed pneumonia due to difficulty in swallowing, and also had a heart attack. *I* received a telephone call from the doctor at the hospital telling me that she was very poorly indeed. She had been transferred back to the main hospital. They didn't think she was going to make it, and said if I wanted to see her I had better go straight away. Apparently her chest was full of blood clots!

David and I went to the hospital immediately. She had been sedated because she had become very distressed and kept shouting and trying to get out of bed. We went to her and prayed for her. After awhile she opened her eyes and recognised us. Thank God, she pulled through, much to the amazement of the doctors and the nurses. A couple of weeks later she was transferred back for rehabilitation again. Our God is faithful.

The staff at the rehabilitation ward worked very hard trying to get her to walk with the aid of a hoist. She had speech therapy as well. The physiotherapists and the doctors said she would never walk again, and trained her to use an electric wheelchair.

The social worker was a very nice person, but she wanted to put my dear sister in an old people's home. Mary was only sixty-two then and thought she was still young. I knew she wouldn't be able to cope with life in an old people's home so I suggested sheltered accommodation, with carers coming in would be a better option for her.

It just so happened that there was a brand new block of sheltered flats that had only just been built and was due to open very soon. Would we like to go and look at it? Yes please, we certainly would. It proved to be the perfect place for her. She had lived there for over four years now and has settled in well, although she doesn't mix with the other residents, preferring to stay in her flat. She will go down if there is a special dinner like for the Diamond Jubilee for example, but otherwise no. I take her out sometimes if the weather is nice, and David and I have taken her away on holiday as well, which she really enjoys.

One day, when she was in a sort of half way house, while waiting for the sheltered flat to be opened, I discovered she could stand quite well, so I decided to try to get her to walk. With the help of her wheelchair not the electric one, that came later, and my support, she managed to walk a few steps across the room. Every time I went to see her we tried walking and I gave her a walking stick to help, which worked quite well. I was so proud of her, and she was very pleased with herself. One day the physiotherapists visited while I was there and I showed them how Mary was progressing with walking. They were very pleased and from then on they also gave her walking practice. She still hasn't the confidence to walk alone as she has arthritis in her knees and one of them threatens to give way at times, but she will always walk a little if I am with her. If I take her out in the car she will always walk from the car to the cafe or toilet. I always try to take her where she doesn't have to walk far. This not only gives her confidence, but gives her a little exercise as well.

As I said before, she was always there when I needed her, and now I am there for her as she needs me. Funny how those words of promise written over forty years ago turned out to be prophetic.

I initially wrote this account in a notebook in long-hand. I write quite small and had made many alterations, where I suddenly remembered something and wrote it on a separate piece of paper and then stuck it in where it should have been. After this happening several times I began to wonder if anyone other than me would be able to read it in the right order.

One Friday I said to David that I wished I hadn't got rid of my mother's old typewriter. It was built like a tank but it worked ok. I had just presumed it it was not possible to get a new ribbon for it anymore.

The very next day I popped in to my neighbour as I hadn't seen her for a couple of weeks. She had very kindly offered the use of her computer for my writing as we only had a netbook computer ourselves now and no printer, but I hadn't yet taken her up on it. We were chatting over a cup of tea when she suddenly asked me if I would like a typewriter. Had I heard her correctly? Apparently she had been visiting her parents the previous day and her father had asked her if she knew anyone who might like a typewriter as they no longer needed it. "I think it's electric", she said. Wow, I think the Lord must have been listening when I mentioned to David, only the day before, that I wished I still had mother's. "Yes please". I said, and told her about discarding mother's old one, and wishing I had kept it. What are the chances of that happening? Pretty remote, I should think. Another blessing from the Lord? Almost certainly.

Is the Lord's faithfulness Great? Most definitely. Praise Him and bless His glorious name for ever.

www.ingramcontent.com/pod-product-compliance
Ingram Content Group UK Ltd.
Pitfield, Milton Keynes, MK11 3LW, UK
UKHW041824080725
460569UK00001B/9

9 781481 788632